Seasons of the Moon
SUMMER MOON

Seasons of the Moon

SUMMER MOON

JEAN CRAIGHEAD GEORGE

■ HARPERTROPHY®

AN IMPRINT OF HARPERCOLLINS*PUBLISHERS*

Harper Trophy® is a registered trademark
of HarperCollins Publishers Inc.

Summer Moon
Copyright © 2002 by Julie Productions, Inc.
Originally published as individual volumes:
The Moon of the Fox Pups text copyright © 1969, 1992
by Jean Craighead George
The Moon of the Wild Pigs text copyright © 1968, 1992
by Jean Craighead George
The Moon of the Mountain Lions text copyright © 1969, 1991
by Jean Craighead George

Library of Congress Cataloging-in-Publication Data
George, Jean Craighead, 1919–
    Summer moon / Jean Craighead George.—1st Harper Trophy ed.
        p.   cm. — (Seasons of the moon ; 4)
    Works originally published from 1968–1969 in series: The Thirteen
moons.
    Includes bibliographical references.
    Contents: The moon of the fox pups — The moon of the wild pigs —
The moon of the mountain lions.
    ISBN 0-06-440995-3 (pbk.)
    1. Foxes—Juvenile literature.   2. Peccaries—Juvenile literature.
3. Puma—Juvenile literature.   4. Summer—Juvenile literature.
[1. Foxes.   2. Peccaries.   3. Desert animals.   4. Puma.]   I. Title.
QL737.C22 G45   2002   2001024642
599.14'3—dc21   CIP
                                                                AC

Book design by Andrea Vandergrift
❖
First Harper Trophy edition, 2002
Visit us on the World Wide Web!
www.harperchildrens.com

CONTENTS

WHY IS THIS SERIES CALLED
SEASONS OF THE MOON?

Each year there are either thirteen full or thirteen new moons. This series is named in honor of the four seasons of the thirteen moons of the year.

Our culture, which bases its calendar year on sun-time, has no names for the thirteen moons. I have named the thirteen lunar months after thirteen North American animals. Primarily night prowlers, these animals, at a particular time of the year in a particular place, do wondrous things. The places are known to you, but the animal moon names are not because I made them up. So that you can place them on our sun calendar, I have identified them with the names of our months. When I ran out of these, I gave the thirteenth moon, the Moon of the Moles, the expandable name December–January.

Fortunately, the animals do not need calendars, for names or no names, sun-time, or moon-time, they follow their own inner clocks.

—JEAN CRAIGHEAD GEORGE

THE MOON OF THE FOX PUPS

One after another the trees of North America paraded into flower and leaf. The first to color the gray landscapes of the Northeast were the willows. They were followed by the maples, then aspens, wild cherries, tulip trees, elms, dogwoods, sycamores, and beeches. Each tree had its own biological alarm clock that told it when to flower and leaf. The last to bear leaves were the oaks. Their bronze leaflets burst from their buds, unfolded, and turned green. And then it was June.

Bees hummed. Young bluebirds fluttered out of their nests to the excited cries of their parents. Baby blue jays perched on tree limbs without falling, and crows sneaked through branches to feed their blue-eyed young waiting for them in nests made of sticks. Rain-filled brooks tinkled over the eggs of bass and trout, and the petals of the fruit trees blew away. Dandelions turned silver, cherries ripened; and from dens and hollows, the children of the woods peered out upon a June-green world. The moon of growing up was upon the land.

Among the peekers were five bright-eyed fox pups. It was early evening, about six o'clock. The fox pups were in the entrance of their den at the edge of a woods, staring out at a farm in the Cumberland Valley of Pennsylvania. Across the United States and Canada, from mountain to plain to forest, red foxes live in patches of cover near open spaces where they can hunt mice and small game.

The farm by the Callapasink Creek was a

perfect fox habitat. Woods grew along the stream and over the hills. A meadow surrounded a coin-round pond and a vegetable garden. Wooden fences marked off open fields of wheat, corn, and alfalfa.

The fox den was on the wooded hillside above the creek, just far enough back among the trees so as not to be visible to the people, but not so far that the foxes could not keep their eyes on these hunter-neighbors. Last year the fox parents had enlarged and lived in an old woodchuck hole, but this spring they had dug their own den. When it was completed, they called to each other in many high-pitched *wurps* that sounded like human laughter.

On this evening the pups, ears up, black noses wet and shining, were watching and waiting for their parents at the mouth of the den.

A warm wind stirred the whorl of leaves on an Indian cucumber root, a perky wildflower. All the fox pups turned their heads to watch it dance. A June beetle alighted heavily on the flowers of a wild leek plant. All heads turned its way. A yellow star grass dropped a petal. Five pairs of eyes studied it.

A moment later a red-winged blackbird settled on a fragile iris blooming by the creek. The pups cocked their heads and watched the bird. He lost his footing and fluttered down to a yellow mass of swamp buttercups. His mate, who was brooding their newly hatched nestlings in the reeds near the iris, cheeped softly. The pups listened.

A robin flew off the nest she had built of mud and sticks among the white flowers of a wild rose bush. She darted over the fox den. Flying as far as the patch of pale wood sorrel, she dropped a small white object. It was a fecal sac, a little bag of body wastes held in a membrane. She had received it from a nestling. Parent songbirds pick up these bags and carry them far away to keep the nest site clean. The robin circled home, flying low over the blooming whorled loosestrife and the fragrant yellow bells of the spreading dogbane.

The fox pups scanned the distant fields. The farmer was coming home on his tractor. He had been cultivating corn all day.

Suddenly all five pairs of black, fur-trimmed ears swiveled to the right. A wild geranium had rustled. The leaves of a Christmas fern whispered, and the pups' regal father stepped onto a rock. His red fur shone; his black nose, legs, and tail glistened. His belly fur swung white and soft. The ferns whispered again. The graceful mother stood beside her mate.

The dog fox and the vixen scanned the land for enemies, sensed the rightness of the moment, and signaled to the pups. Theirs was a silent signal—just a twitch of their tails. Having called, they started down the hill. Quietly the pups followed.

For the first time the fox pups ran beyond

their play yard, a trampled four-by-six-foot area in front of the den. They tumbled over one another in their eagerness to be in the midst of all they had seen—fluttering blackbirds, June beetles, busy robins.

The pups were nine weeks old. One was a male; the other four were females. Their parents had mated in February, and seven and a half weeks later, in early April, the pups were born. They had been well furred on the first day of life. Their eyes opened ten days later, and they prowled the tunnel. They saw their mother. They stared at her, taking in her shape and face. Finally they saw one another. They whimpered soft greetings.

Although the pups could see, they were still quite helpless. They wobbled when they walked, on legs with bones so delicate they seemed like fragile glass. They still nursed, and they could not clean and groom their fur. They needed their mother constantly, and so their father brought her food. He dropped mice, meadow voles, and rabbits near the den's entrance, for these were the main foods of the foxes, who also eat wild black cherries, a few birds, salamanders, and frogs, in season. Grasshoppers are fox snacks in August and September, as well as apples, blackberries, or an occasional bite of fresh corn.

One day after the pups' eyes opened, the father came partway into the dimly lit tunnel. Fifteen feet back into the hill, the fox pups heard him. They approached him gingerly, sensing his importance. Having introduced himself, he went away.

As the days passed, the biological clocks inside the pups ticked on, and as they did, they were able to do new things: yip, box, and roll onto their backs. They ate less often. They were awake longer. They were ready to be left alone for several hours, and so the vixen took off to go hunting and to lounge in the sun.

When they were five weeks of age, and stable on their feet, the mother led them up the long tunnel to the entrance of the den. They looked out on the beautiful woodland and farm. Their father lay curled on a nearby rock. He watched cannily for enemies while the pups ventured into the play yard. For hours they smelled plants and rolled pebbles with their paws. When they stumbled with fatigue, the vixen led them back into the den and nursed them.

The next night she began their schooling. She brought a dead mouse to the play yard. At first they stared at it, then sniffed it, and finally the male reached out and touched it. He barked a high-pitched *weirp*. A sister bit his tail. He turned and bit her tail, then chased his own. Another sister grabbed the mouse. The male knocked her over with his shoulder. She pounced on him, and the mouse was forgotten as the pups boxed and tumbled. The moon of

June was moving on, and the clocks of the pups had arrived at "play." They had also arrived at "knowledge." The male pup knew what a mouse was. He had eaten one.

The nights and days revolved. The pups grew on. One evening they were able to scratch behind their ears instead of in the air. A few nights later they reared and pounced in the manner of the fox. With that, their father dragged a dead mouse across the ground and hid it under the leaves. They tracked it down by scent. Just before dawn, lifting their heads into the wind, they picked out the odors of the cattle and the people on the air. Their clocks had ticked to "smell."

Now they were ready to follow the dog fox and vixen into the woods and fields. And so this evening, after watching the blackbird, the beetle, and the robin, they ran out of their play yard and followed their parents into the bigger world.

At the bottom of the hill their father, the dog fox, halted. The vixen stopped in her tracks; but the pups, who were not yet coordinated, bumped into their parents' tails and one another before finally braking to a stop. Their father was pointing with his nose to something on the ground. A box turtle, head and legs inside her bony carapace, was settled on the earth. Her shell was closed. The dog fox picked her up and placed the stonelike reptile among his pups. The pups cocked their ears and sniffed her. This was no mouse. The turtle opened her "door" slightly. A pup nosed her, and the door shut on the little wet nose. The pup yelped in pain. The other pups drew back in respect. Satisfied that his offspring knew a box turtle, the dog fox turned and trotted toward the stream. The family followed stealthily.

The turtle, using the earth as a sounding board, waited until the vibrations from the fox steps died away. Then she opened her shell, thrust out her feet and hard, blunt head, and walked. She went back to the spot where the fox had picked her up and began to dig with strong, slow thrusts of her hind feet and claws. She made a hole about four inches deep. In this she laid six leathery eggs, then pushed the loam back over them. In the earth nest the eggs would slowly develop, until, on some cool night about October first, the little turtles would break out of their shells and struggle up to the woodland floor.

The eggs laid, the turtle thumped away, not remembering the day in May when she had been the object of a fierce and noisy turtle battle. On that day a male had found her eating wild-lily bulbs. He tapped her shell with his bony chest plate and invited her to be his mate. At that moment another turtle came around a stone and lumbered toward the pair. He desired the female, too. The first male struck his rival with his nose. He struck again, and then, with resounding blows, thumped him with his chest and head until his own nose was bleeding. Finally he turned the rival onto his back in ignominious turtle defeat. Then he knocked on the female's shell once more, and she accepted him. Now, at twilight in the month of June, she had laid her eggs and left them for the earth to incubate.

The swift-footed foxes followed the stream shore to the meadow. The dog fox paused and crouched. A fat young woodchuck was eating grass beneath a sycamore tree. He had been born on the same day as the fox pups, but he had developed faster than they. When he was only four weeks old, he came out of the den to eat clover and grass. Two weeks later when his mother's milk dried up, she drove him and his two sisters from the burrow. She was done with rearing them. They were on their own.

The young chuck had walked away from his mother, but then turned back. She threatened him again, and this time he ran. He sped among silver dandelion heads to the flowering meadow, far from his mother. Here he dug himself a burrow and lived in peace until this moment.

Now he was frightened—the dog fox was stalking him. The young woodchuck was about to scurry down his burrow when the fox stood up, lifted his head, and walked away.

The woodchuck went back to his meal of clover, unaware that the dog fox and the vixen were scheming against him. She was crouched in the weeds, just out of his sight. Suddenly, with a dancer's grace, she leaped out of the grass and took him in her mouth. One shake and he was senseless, but by no means dead. The vixen carried him to her pups to show them this fox food.

The young male picked him up and lifted him high. A sister snatched him away, and he charged her. Regaining his senses, the chuck rolled swiftly to his four short legs, stood up, and growling, slashed out with his sharp rodent teeth. Five surprised pups learned the fury of the woodchuck before he dashed into his burrow.

The parents did not chase the chuck, for there were other lessons to be taught. The dog fox switched his tail and led his family into the orchard.

Under an apple tree he paused and glanced up into the branches. The orange breast of a male northern oriole glowed among the small green apples as the bird threw back his head and sang his beautiful song to the evening. The dog fox passed right on by him to say that the oriole was not food.

In an elm tree nearby the mother oriole was incubating eggs in a soft gray basket she had made from fibers stripped from thready milkweed and grapevine stems. The nest had taken her six days to build. On the first day she had made a circle of threads in a fork of the tree. Next she began to weave, flying around and around the circle, pushing fibers in and out until she had an open-toed "sock." She wiggled inside the sock and closed the toe with her weavings. As she worked, she chirped to herself.

Occasionally her mate brought her threads for the nest, but for the most part, he just sang. By the time of the crescent moon of June, the female had finished her nest and laid her full clutch of eggs, one each morning for five days. Then she incubated them. The male stayed nearby as if to encourage her in her lonely task. The fox pups did not see the nest high above their heads on the drooping tip of a limb.

They came to a puddle in the lane. With a burst of white wings, a hundred cabbage butterflies flew up into the air. The fox pups *wurp*ed and chased them among the daisies. The vixen circled the bouncing pups and rounded them up like naughty sheep. They were too frolicsome. The goshawk would see them and attack. Herding them to their father, she snarled until they crouched in silence. One by one the butterflies dropped back to the puddle. A few, however, flitted off to the garden. In the moist evening air they alighted on the cabbages and searched for sheltered spots to lay their eggs.

The fox family arrived at the edge of the creek. The pups had never been so close to rushing water, and they stared at it curiously. Boldly, the young male stuck in his nose and sniffed. He yelped in pain, sneezed, and pawed his face. Sitting down, he looked at his father for an explanation. The dog fox trotted to the creek edge and lapped. The young male lapped, too.

A catbird in the willows heard the fox pup yelp. With a cry, he flew to a twig in full view of the family, vibrated his wings, flicked his long gray tail, and hopped a little higher. He was distracting their attention from his mate and five fat youngsters, who were cuddled in a nest of sticks in the greenbrier patch.

The little birds were five days old, and like the pups, they were growing up. Just this morning they had attempted to preen their feathers for the first time. They had also yawned. Until this day they could do very little—just lie on their bellies, open their mouths, and defecate in little sacs like the robins. Tomorrow, according to their inner clocks, they would stand for the first time. On the seventh day they would lift their wings up and spread them to the side. On the tenth day they would shake themselves. On the eleventh day they would leave the nest and sit on twigs in the brier patch.

Here they would hop, jump, flutter, and walk up stalks. They would make short flights. On the twelfth day they would sleep with their bills in their back feathers, and on the thirteenth day they would be able to pick up food in their beaks, wag their tails, and drink. A day later they would have developed so far, they would be able to give the alarm call of the cat-bird. On and on they would grow in bird skills, until by September they would be as independent as their parents. In October they would fly south to Florida and the shores of the Gulf of Mexico for the winter. It takes a long time to grow.

The five pups watched the scolding, flapping catbird just as he wanted them to do, and so they did not see his nest in the greenbrier patch, nor would they have been interested if they had. Foxes prefer mice to songbirds, although they would take a bird if it fell before them. Mice are easier to catch.

The dog fox called his family and they trotted along the creek shore. Still not master of his feet, the male pup made an unpardon-able fox error. He snapped a stick. The sound frightened a mallard duck who had brought her brood under the drooping willow limbs to spend the night. She squawked, and streaked out across the surface of the water. Fifteen downy ducklings followed, a huge family. The mother had incubated not only her own ten eggs, but five more. A young female, confused by the excitement of the May egg-laying time, had deposited her eggs in the wrong nest. This did not matter to the older mother. She simply incubated and hatched them all. Now she was herding them all across the creek, far from the duck-eating foxes.

When darkness came, the dog fox led his family to the farmhouse. They smelled the barn swallows under the eaves of the porch. The young birds had been flying over and around the farm catching insects all day. Before dusk they had come home to roost for the night, even though their mother was incubating a second clutch of eggs. They settled down in the eaves not far from her. She did not chase them away as the mother woodchuck had done, for the barn swallows are cooperative birds. The first babies help to feed the second round of hungry mouths.

The moon came up. It lit the flowering heads of the wheat and the foot-high blades of corn. The fox pups followed their parents past the fields and along the side of the barn where a day-old calf lay with its mother. They stumbled from weariness. Quick to sense their needs, the vixen led them back to the den, leaving her mate to hunt food for them all.

The next evening the pups were full of energy. They rolled and tumbled in the play yard while they waited for their parents to take them out again. A bullfrog croaked from the edge of the farm pond, then another croaked, and another. June is the breeding season for these, the latest frogs of the Northeast to sing and lay their eggs. They sounded like mournful bassoons.

Presently the father fox came up the hill

and led the pups to the pond. The vixen ran beside him. At the water's edge he skirted grass and reeds until he found a delicious bullfrog. Rearing to his hind legs, he leaped, missed, and frightened the amphibian. It dove into the water with a splash, to the excitement of the little foxes. They ran around the pond scaring the big frogs and learning their habits.

As many skills as the puppies now had, they still had to learn the more subtle sounds of the woods and field. One night by the creek they saw their father twist his ears to say he had heard a noise. They listened, but the marsh was quiet. A furry nose appeared in a hole not two feet from them. A young muskrat rushed out of his den, gnashing his teeth as his mother chased him. The moon of growing up had cast its spell. Like the woodchuck's mother, his mother was making it quite clear that it was time for her offspring to go seek his fortune.

The young muskrat did not look back at

her. He closed his nostrils and dove into the water. So upset was he that he did not even see the foxes watching him. He swam until he reached the other shore, then pulled up on the embankment and rested. Nearby, another homeless juvenile was eating cattail fruits. They set out together to explore the creek; and by the night's end, both had forgotten their mothers and were digging homes of their own.

As the moon was beginning to wane, the fox pups were chewing old bones, sticks, stones, acorns. Their baby teeth were falling out, their sharp adult ones coming in. They chewed whatever they found. One evening when the male pup bit his father too hard while playing, the dog fox got to his feet and swished his tail. It was time for the pups to hunt, not just look.

The dog fox and the vixen began the hunting lessons by chasing mice to the pups, or scaring a rabbit their way. After many misses the pups were finally successful, and their growls became deeper and more serious.

One night the young male fox came upon the warm trail of a meadow vole. Legs flying, nose in the wind, he raced along its scent. A mother pheasant, incubating her eight olive-brown eggs, listened in alarm as he came toward her. She pressed herself tightly against her eggs and sat perfectly still, as if frozen. The pup did not see the pheasant. He ran right past her, and caught the vole at the bottom of a fence post.

The next night was hot. The foxes stayed within the coolness of the earth, but the insects crept and flew. Their season of greatest activity was just beginning. In the grasses young crickets crawled. They had recently hatched from eggs in the soil, and although they looked much like their parents, with their long antennae and big heads, they were still growing up.

The young crickets could not sing. It would be August before they would fill the day and night with chirps. Occasionally, however, one tried. A young cricket lifted its stubby wings. The musical instrument of the cricket is a file on the edge of one wing, which is rubbed against a saw on the other. This makes only a small sound, so within the wing of every cricket is an amplifier, a megaphone-shaped box, that enlarges the minute scraping noise into a blast.

The young male fox saw the young cricket near the den door and came out to see what it was. He nosed him. The cricket scurried under a leaf. The pup did not pursue him, for a new scent was on the wind. He didn't know what the scent was, but it made his mouth water. He traced it to the bottom of the hill. There he learned that strawberries are delicious.

As the fox pups learned to hunt, their mother's milk diminished, and she, like the woodchuck and muskrat, became quite irritable when her offspring begged for milk. One night she snapped at the male fox pup. He backed away, turned, and ran down the hill. He had never left his family group before; but tonight was different. He felt comfortable on his own.

He trotted to the stream. He was not as round and fat as he had been when the quarter moon had risen. His legs were longer, and he did not tumble when he walked. He was a graceful juvenile fox.

Beneath an oak he stopped. Something had sailed through the limbs. It sailed back. His sharp eyes picked out the shape of a small flying squirrel among the leaves. Gray, with a flattened tail and large eyes, and trimmed with velvet black, the pretty animal saw the fox, gathered his feet under him, and leaped. He spread his front and hind legs. Membranes covered with fur made "sails" between his wrists and ankles, and he soared off into the night. A limb was in his way. The young squirrel reefed in his right sail and swerved around the limb, lost altitude, and alighted at the bottom of a maple. He ran to the top of the tree and sailed off again.

Born in an old woodpecker hole at the end of March, the flying squirrel had come into the world feeble and naked. His eyes had not opened for twenty-eight days. A week later he had been weaned, and in another week, like the fox pups, he had followed his mother into the woods. He had an inner clock, too, and when he was eight weeks old he made his first short glide. Now an expert at this mode of travel, he flew off through the woods to hunt seeds and nuts.

The juvenile fox leaped silently over a log and glided up the creek shore. On a sycamore trunk he came upon two big cecropia moths quivering their wings. They are the largest of the North American moths. The male had followed a scent of the female for three miles before finding her. In a few days she would lay her eggs and die. The life of a moth is not long.

The juvenile looked curiously at the

beautiful moths and walked on. They were not fox food. He came to the creek and, stepping into the water, walked in deeper and deeper until he was swimming. He circled a pool, then came ashore. Shaking off the water, he pulled a wet leaf from his chest and licked his legs and feet dry. He was at last old enough to clean and groom his fur.

The moon of June had waxed and waned. Its dark side faced the earth. Twenty-seven and a third days had passed since the June moon had appeared in the sky. Although the night was dark, the juvenile fox saw well with his yellow, light-gathering eyes. He saw the bats escort their young out of the farmhouse attic and over the pond to catch insects. He saw the newly hatched fish in the shallows spread out across the bottom to sleep. In the trees he saw the male fireflies glow as they called to the females in the grass. All these sights lured the young fox to continue.

From now on he would see his family less and less until finally, in autumn, he would take off in a straight line across the country. He would travel perhaps a hundred miles to find a patch of cover near open spaces where he would live out his life.

The young fox trotted along the creek shore, around the pond, and off across the meadow. He investigated the fields on the next farm. The moon of growing up was done.

THE MOON OF THE WILD PIGS

In the blazing heat of July, a wild piglet stood alone in the desert. He was lost and squealing for his clan. His cry did not travel far, for the hot air muted his voice. It carried only to the big red rock several yards from where he was standing. There it faded and died in the heat.

The temperature was already above 100 degrees Fahrenheit, and it was not yet noontime. Not a cloud shielded the desert from the fire of the sun, for the moon of July was upon the Northern Hemisphere, the moon of heat and dryness.

July is not only the hottest and driest time

of the year, it is also a time of violent thunderstorms and lightning. Nowhere are these factors more extreme in the United States and Mexico than on the Great American Desert.

The Great American Desert is made up of four parts: the Great Basin, or Sage, Desert of Colorado, Wyoming, Arizona, and California; the Mojave of California and Arizona; the Sonoran Desert of Arizona, Baja California, and Sonora, Mexico; and the Chihuahuan Desert of New Mexico, Texas, and part of Mexico.

Deserts make up one seventh of the planet's land surface. By definition they are areas that receive ten inches or less of rain per year. Many deserts receive almost no rain. Some are lifeless; others support sparse numbers of drought-adapted plants and animals. A desert can be cold and dry like the tundra of Siberia, or hot and dry like the Sonoran Desert of Arizona, where the piglet lived.

The little creature was very young. He still wore his reddish coat with a black stripe down his back. He was a peccary, a pig unique to the Americas. A peccary is neither a wild boar nor a domestic pig, both of which were introduced from Eurasia, but is related to both.

Certain differences set the peccaries apart from their relatives. Pigs have many young at one time, the peccary usually has two. Pigs have four toes on each hind foot, peccaries have three. Peccaries have musk glands on their backs above their tails, pigs do not. Not much more than a yard long and a little less than two feet high, adult peccaries weigh at the most fifty pounds, as compared to one hundred fifty pounds for domestic pigs. Unlike the tail of a domestic pig, a peccary's tail is barely visible. A collar of pale bristles around its neck gives this wild pig the name "collared peccary." Although in the United States peccaries live in the brush-lands of Texas, Arizona, and New Mexico, they are most abundant in the Sonoran Desert. Heat, scarce water, spiny plants, and deadly creatures are as normal to a peccary as a meadow to a meadowlark.

The piglet was two months old. He could have been born any month of the year, for peccaries have no special season for giving birth. He and his sister happened to have been born in May. Consequently he did not know about the extremes of the moon of July.

He stood in a remarkable landscape. The tops of purple mountains rose above him like piles of broken glass. In the valleys, giant saguaro cacti speared the sky like enormous green stick men with uplifted arms. Creosote and mesquite bushes huddled at their bases. Arroyos, or dry riverbeds, streaked the slopes with debris from the flash floods of summer.

The hour was now past noon, the time of day when peccaries are asleep in caves or under bushes. But not this piglet. He was wide-awake and sniffing the hot air, trying to find his mother and his clan.

Until half an hour ago he had been sleeping under a mesquite bush with his clan of nine members—old, young, and adolescent. Peccaries go foraging in the cool hours of dawn and dusk. During the heat of the day they retreat to caves or the shade of bushes. The strong-smelling bush where the piglet's clan rested was on the bank of the Santa Cruz Wash in Arizona, a waterless arroyo for most of the year. From this and other resting sites they wandered far, grubbing for food—the fruits of the cacti, nuts, beans, herbs, roots, insects, and, when they could find them, the eggs of birds. Occasionally in the moon of July they sought a distant water hole, but most of the time they did not need to drink. Peccaries eat the watery pads of the prickly-pear cactus.

When the merciless sun came up this morning, the peccary clan retreated to the mesquite above the dry river. Just before noon the large gray peccary boar arose and lifted his head. He sniffed the winds from the south and rattled his tusks, canine teeth that are used for communicating and occasionally digging and fighting. This morning he was rattling out a warning. The other two adult boars got to their feet, sniffed, and rattled their tusks. The piglet's mother clattered her teeth.

Hearing the warnings, the piglet scampered under his mother's belly and looked out from between her legs. He could see nothing to fear. No enemies were in sight: not the mountain lion or the coyote or the bobcat. The mourning doves called softly. No piglet-eating eagles sailed the white-hot sky.

The boar, however, who was wise to desert scents, had smelled a thunderstorm. It was moving swiftly toward the foot of the Tucson Mountains, where he and his clan were huddled. He could not see the storm on the horizon, for he was nearsighted, but he could smell it, and he knew what to do.

He rubbed his musk gland against another boar to exchange odors. Then he rubbed the piglet's mother and the adolescents. They all in turn rubbed their glands on the gray boar, the piglet, and one another. When all the scents were mixed, the clan smelled different from all other clans. If the storm separated them, as one often did, or if they were separated by an enemy, the clan odor would bring them together again.

Then the gray boar grunted and led the group out of the shade, down the volcanic rocks, and up the middle of the arroyo. They all followed quickly except the piglet. All the tooth rattling had made him reluctant to leave the brush. His mother urged his sister to follow another sow and ran back for the piglet. She bunted him up the arroyo with her long, pointed nose. He fought her until he reached the enormous red rock that split the arroyo into two arroyos. There a spiny lizard darted out from under a clump of brown, brittle grass. The piglet scampered after it, his cloven hoofs clinking on the hot stones. He followed the lizard down one of the two arroyos. Its ripples and eddies were hot sand, its waterfalls cracked clay. At a large greenish stone the lizard disappeared. The piglet searched for it, then gave up and turned around. Every member of his clan had disappeared.

This did not frighten him. His clan would come and get him. They always did when he trotted off. So devoted and gentle were they to him and to one another that the piglet could not imagine life without them. So he didn't. He sat down and waited.

He had come by this sense of companionship early in life. Two hours after his birth in a clump of mesquite, he had been on his feet nursing. A day later he and his sister, who were about the size of rabbits, had followed their mother up the mountain. A massive gray boar had greeted him with a sniff, then rubbed his musk on him. The boar then had sniffed and rubbed the piglet's sister.

One by one all the members of his clan had sniffed, rubbed, and accepted the piglets. Two adult females had nosed and mothered them, and the warm feeling of clan comradery had been born that day in the piglet.

From that moment until the clan had rattled their teeth at the thunderstorm, he had not known fear.

He had been uncomfortable once. His mother had grunted to warn him of the cholla cactus, known as the "jumping cactus" for good reason. It is made up of twiglike joints covered with sharp spines. They break off at the slightest touch and fairly leap onto the passerby. Having been warned to avoid this plant, the curious piglet had nevertheless walked right up to it and been instantly covered with clumps of piercing spines. He had squealed and run in circles until his mother had dislodged the cholla joints with her feet and teeth.

Now he felt another sort of discomfort—aloneness. He sniffed to find the scent of his clan. The air was too hot and dry to hold it. He lowered his head to find his own scent and follow it back to the red rock. It, too, had burned off in the heat. The desert air was now well above 100 degrees Fahrenheit and still getting hotter. The piglet crept into the shade of a paloverde tree and waited to be rescued.

A true desert tree, this spreading plant adjusts to the heat and dryness by dropping its leaves so that water is not lost by evaporation, a process called transpiration in plants. The paloverde stays alive by manufacturing chlorophyll with its green bark.

Near the piglet grew another plant that had dropped its leaves to survive the drought of July, the ocotillo. It also adapts to the desert in another way. Like the winter trees in the north, it becomes dormant, its leafless stems clustered like gray pencils in a cup against the hot yellows and oranges of the clay and lava.

The sun disappeared behind a storm cloud. The desert grew dark. Darkness at noon was not right. The piglet got to his feet.

Thunderstorms rumbled over other parts of the country. They blackened the skies in the mid-central states, where the field corn was coming into tassel. They chased cultivators, who were weeding cotton rows for the last time this year, into sheds and houses. They gathered over potato diggers in New Jersey, who were harvesting the first crop of the season, and sent them under cover.

July was also the moon of the insects. From Texas to southern Canada, grasshoppers tried new wings. Bees and wasps buzzed in the warm air. Butterflies flew from flower to flower, and at dusk in the Northeast, fireflies flicked their lights on and off as they spiraled to the tops of the trees. Caterpillars chewed, beetles clicked, bugs bit.

Beneath the paloverde, the piglet listened to the insects. Suddenly they stopped making sounds. The dark noon was too hot for even the hardy insects to stridulate. Frightened, the piglet set out to find his clan. He tripped over a rock and it rolled down the slope into the arroyo. The noise frightened a cactus wren from her nest, an enormous pile of grass she had miraculously placed in a cholla cactus without pricking herself. Her young of the year were on their own, and she was protecting herself from the fire of July by sitting inside her shady, cool home. Seeing only a piglet out in the heat, and warned by the darkness, she returned to her nest.

The low light and heat were pressing down on the piglet like a heavy metal coat. He slowed down and stopped. A commotion overhead caught his attention. He looked up but did not see a Gila woodpecker, unique to the Sonoran Desert, alight on a huge saguaro cactus. The cactus was fifty feet tall and two hundred years old. Saguaro cacti, like all cacti, have adapted to the desert. When it rains, they take up water through their web of roots and store it in their accordionlike trunks, which expand. The trunks contract as the water is used up. This old saguaro was shriveled and almost waterless. The drought had been long.

Hardly had the woodpecker alighted at the hole when she squawked and flew away. An elf owl, who was nesting in the woodpecker's hole of last year, had frightened her. The tiny owl, no more than three inches high, was sheltering her two young under her feathers. Seeing the woodpecker, she had snapped her beak and spread her wings over her face, then peered out through the feathers like a demon.

This was the elf owl's way of scaring off an enemy, and it was very successful. The woodpecker did not come back.

The storm closed in on the mountain. The piglet trudged on in search of his clan. When he came to a boulder almost as big as the red rock, he hesitated, then turned west. A cluster of desert marigolds bobbed in the small breeze he created in passing. Most of the wildflowers of the desert bloom in March after the soft winter rains. Briefly and brilliantly they flower, and swiftly they make seeds that do not need water. As seeds they survive the moon of July.

The piglet stepped over a rock and surprised a male tarantula, the largest of the North American spiders, the female being almost as big as a man's fist. The spider peered up at the piglet with beady eyes and opened his jaws to strike.

The piglet might have trampled the hairy creature to death with his front feet as he had seen his mother do, but he was in a hurry to find his clan. The blackness was now rumbling.

The spider was two years old, the age for a tarantula to seek a mate. For several nights he had been roaming over miles of desert looking for one of the larger and tempestuous females of his species. He searched with both boldness and caution, for it requires enormous skill to court a female tarantula.

First he must tease her until she becomes angry enough to attack him. Then, as she raises her poison fangs to kill, he must grab those fangs with his front feet and hold them tightly while he slips his special feet, on which he carries his life code, into pockets on her abdomen. Having managed that, he is still not out of trouble. He must let go and escape before she kills him, which sometimes happens.

The male tarantula went courting by night, but any disturbance inspired him to check to see if it were a mate. The clang of the piglet's hoofs had brought him out of his hole dug into the soil, to see who was there. He did not go far. Crackling lightning sent him back to his den.

The piglet squealed at the sight of the lightning bolts. A boom of thunder drowned out his cry. He squealed again and lay down. Under the earth a round-tailed ground squirrel was asleep for the duration of the moons of July and August. She and her family spent the hot months in the dormant state of estivation—summer sleep.

The cool earth was a retreat for many desert animals. Scorpions, mice, foxes, squirrels, bats, and even owls moved about in underground tunnels, runways, and living quarters. Dainty kit foxes, not much bigger than house cats, played inside round earthen hollows, trampled to smoothness by their feet. Pregnant rattlesnakes coiled in burrows, waiting for August when they would not lay eggs, but give birth to live young as some snakes do. Scorpions hid in fox burrows, and burrowing owls took up quarters in the ground squirrels' chambers.

Banner-tailed kangaroo rats were also staying cool underground, even though they are better adapted to heat and drought than most desert animals. The big-eyed, soft-furred mammals never drink. Their bodies metabolize the dry seeds they eat and make water. They do not pant or perspire. They rarely urinate.

The jackrabbit battled the desert heat yet another way. He has long ears and legs. The more surface area an animal has, the more heat leaves its body. The jackrabbit's ears and legs were his air conditioners.

The thunder rolled, a wind came up, and the piglet cried for his clan. Although peccaries are often led by a sow, they don't have a dominant leader as wolves or monkeys do. They follow an individual for his or her talent. The gray boar had an excellent sense of smell; the piglet's mother had keen ears; other members of the group were experts on where to find roots or mesquite beans. This made for a secure and relaxed group.

Once their young are born, the females simply go about their business, and the little ones follow and learn. Sows often take the sentinel watch while the clan sleeps. When hunters, lions, or dogs are smelled, the sentinels raise the bristles on their backs and clash their teeth. This may send the clan deeper into a cave or disperse them in all directions. Spread out, they are more difficult for enemies to track and kill. When the danger passes, the family scent brings them back together again.

The thunder roared and growled. The piglet lifted his nose and sniffed. The faint scent of his clan was on the air. Even the terrible heat and darkness did not scare him now. He grunted as he followed the odor to a pack-rat nest, a three-foot pile of cholla cactus joints, the sticky enemy of the piglet. The rat had carried home the spine-filled joints by taking each one gingerly in his teeth and dragging it between his front feet. The rat never once touched the spines.

The piglet cautiously circled the rat nest. The scent of his clan was somewhere on this spiny castle. He passed a slingshot, a bottle top, and a road map of Arizona. The rat had woven these found objects into his home.

And then he located the scent. It lay on a single cholla joint that the rat had found along the trail the peccaries had taken to the arroyo. Discouraged, the piglet walked on.

A crackling rattle catapulted him into a prickly-pear thicket. He raised the dark bristles along his spine and rattled his canine teeth. He had disturbed a rattlesnake. Scrambling for a footing, the piglet turned, skidded, then ran full tilt around a mesquite tree and back into the arroyo. He stood still. He could not hear the rattlesnake anymore, so he lay down on his pink belly and stared at the darkening mountainside.

His fear of the rattler had been born two

weeks ago, when the gray boar had come upon just such a deadly tiger rattlesnake. He had clattered his teeth to warn his clan, and they had dispersed, rattling their tusks and throwing the fear of the snake into the piglet. He had run to safety under his mother's belly. Now he had nowhere to go. He trembled.

When he stopped shaking, he realized he was breathing in the scent of his clan once more. Scrambling to his feet, he dashed up the arroyo, only to be disappointed again. The odor was his own. He had traveled in a large circle and was right back where he had started. Before him lay the greenish stone where the lizard had vanished. He whimpered and lay down, fear tingling like fire in his belly. The thunder boomed.

A tiny dragon of the desert was startled by the piglet's footsteps. Covered with spikes and spines and scaly armor, the horned lizard ran a few feet on the hot clay, then stopped. She was heavy with eggs. She would lay them toward the end of the month, and leave them to incubate in the heat. They would hatch in thirty days. As she glanced at the piglet, the rattler came over a rock. The horned lizard rose on her short legs and shot the snake with a stream of blood from her eyes: one of the most bizarre defenses in the entire animal kingdom. It worked. The snake slid off.

The piglet rolled his eyes and cried to his clan. The temperature was 120 degrees, and the heat was painful. He left the arroyo and crept under a mesquite bush.

Two Gambel's quail were resting under the bush. They ran when the piglet approached. The quail were a delicate blue-gray with chestnut sides and a dark tear-shaped plume of feathers curled out from their foreheads. They piped a winsome call, and seven brown-and-yellow chicks no bigger than quarters popped up and followed their parents with the swiftness of shooting stars. They crossed the arroyo and hid with their parents in a cluster of plants. Desert plants seek one another's shade, not the sunshine, and so grow close together.

The piglet's call went unanswered. Tucking his toes under him, putting his head on the ground, he whimpered and waited.

To his surprise he was looking at a road runner on the other side of the mesquite bush, who was looking at him. Her beak was longer than her head, and her tail longer than her body. She was the ground-dwelling member of the cuckoo family and as swift as the automobiles she liked to race. She moved and frightened a lizard, who dashed out of the grass. With the speed of a Cadillac the road runner chased, caught, and ate it. It was too large to swallow, so she sat down to digest the head while the tail hung from her bill. She should have been laying a second brood of eggs, but the heat of this July moon was too severe. She needed all her body liquids to stay alive. The

Norman Adams

The young fox gazes
over the woodland and farm at night.

A mother pheasant hides from the hunting fox.

The fox cubs watch the red-winged blackbird.

An elf owl nests inside the cool cactus.

The peccary piglet lives
in the beautiful but harsh Sonoran desert.

Paul Mirocha

The close-knit peccary clan rests together.

Unlike their mother's,
the lion kittens' coats are still spotted.

Curious about the sea,
the lions walk the beach at dawn.

piglet pressed tighter against the earth.

The next roll of thunder shook the ground. The piglet shivered. A bright-red cardinal flew into the center of a yucca plant and sat still. The mourning doves bleated. Then they, too, were motionless.

The thunder was followed by a roaring wind. The ocotillo bushes rocked like stiff wire. The leafless paloverdes clattered, their fallen leaves flying away like birds. The darkness became blackness, then sizzling light. The piglet shook. Jagged forks of fire shot down from the clouds. Piercing cracks of thunder rocked the earth. The tops of the mountains disappeared. A gray fox darted out of the arroyo and into a burrow. The family of quail flew across the dry river bottom and climbed high up the bank.

The piglet stared as the desert flickered with electric bolts. The thunder drummed without letting up.

Then the rain fell. Great drops as big as the

piglet's hoofs splashed on the hot, dry soil. They fell faster and faster, until the piglet could no longer see beyond the mesquite bush. Drops became sheets, sheets became silver with lightning flashes, and then the devastation began. A flash flood was on its way.

The piglet heard a low whisper. The whisper became a roar as water poured off the mountains into the arroyo. It gathered momentum. Rumbling, it tore up everything in its path—bushes, cacti, animals, boulders—and carried them toward the piglet. He lay still, not knowing what to do.

A bolt of lightning forked with teeth of fire struck a saguaro cactus not fifteen feet away. The piglet jumped in terror and ran up the bank. He dashed through waterfalls and clambered up cascades. Behind him the cactus was aglow. Every spine lit up with electricity—and burned.

The piglet did not look back. He did not

see the torrent of water come down the arroyo, lift the greenish stone where he had just been, and carry it like a stick into the valley. Finally he stopped on a ledge above the red rock—and there was his mother. She was not fifty feet from where he had left her a short time ago.

She and the clan were under an overhang. The gray boar, who had sensed the storm, had been taking them there when the piglet saw the lizard. Now the piglet squealed and ran under his mother's belly.

The storm raged for half an hour, obscuring flats, mountains, and rising arroyos. Five inches of water fell. Then the sun came out. Every rock and hill dripped. Eight-inch-long centipedes emerged from cracks and rocks and rippled along looking for insects to eat. The great saguaro cacti were swelling, as each took up thousands of pounds of water with its webs of roots that lie close to the surface. Leaf buds swelled on the leafless paloverdes, and the dry ocotillo dripped and turned green. Quail, mice, deer, and peccaries drank. Water had come to the desert with the moon of the wild pigs.

Almost as swiftly as it had come, the rain sank into the porous earth and was gone.

The piglet heard sweet piping sounds. The toads had awakened from their torpor. These amphibians cannot live without water. During the drought they were deep in the earth. When the rains wet the soil, they dug swiftly to the surface and began singing. They were in a hurry. They must quickly mate and lay eggs. Their eggs must hatch into pollywogs and the pollywogs turn into toads before the puddles dry up and send them back into the ground for another year, or until the next rain.

That night the moon shone down on a desert of sparse but green plants. It shone on a tired piglet who was snuggled beside his mother and sister in the midst of his friendly peccary clan.

THE MOON OF THE
MOUNTAIN LIONS

The young mountain lion opened his mouth and rolled out his tongue in a waking yawn. Lying in his summer den at timberline, he turned his gaze upon his home on the side of Mount Olympus in Washington. Snowcapped peaks speared the darkness above him. An alpine meadow splattered with flowers lay below, and far down the mountain shaggy forests hugged the slopes and glacial valleys. Below them the northern rain forest reached to the Pacific Ocean.

Stretching and cupping his whiskers forward, the noble cat arose and quietly stepped into the moonlight. He stood beneath the moon of August, the moon of change.

The hummingbirds, sippers of flower nectar, had already sensed the force of this moon. They were ready to migrate. The temperature had dropped only one or two degrees across North America and had actually risen that much on the Pacific Coast, yet the flower birds were ready to go. The sun was setting earlier and rising later. The days were growing shorter. Snow and darkness were coming to the mountains.

At the dawn of this day several male rufous hummingbirds, some of the tiniest birds in the world, had darted past the lion's den as they spun south on whirling wings. No bigger than daisy heads, they were off toward winter homes on the plateaus of Mexico three thousand miles away. Their females stayed behind to hurriedly feed the last brood of nestlings. They would see their bud-sized youngsters out of the nests and onto their wings, teach them how to sip the nectar of the last lilies and bellflowers, then all would follow the males to the sunny winter lands where flowers bloomed.

The swallows also felt the change of the August moon. Great flocks were gathering by the thousands and tens of thousands over lakes, marshes, and seacoasts. Almost always on the wing, these agile birds have tiny, feeble feet that they rarely use. Before the moon would wane they would climb high into the sky and, out of sight of man and beast, circle and rest on their wings. Then, on a cue from the sun, they would turn south and speed away. The next day the swallows would be gone, leaving the skies strangely empty, like beaches when winter comes.

Other animals were responding differently to the change. In the deserts, on the August-dry prairies, and in forests from Mexico up through Canada, the chipmunks, toads, and frogs were asleep. This was not the sleep of hibernation but of estivation, summer's torpor. In this quiet state these animals were avoiding the adversities of the month, dryness and heat.

One beast, however, would combine the sleeps of summer and winter. In the rockslides, the Olympic marmots, the whistlers of high country, were getting ready for the longest sleep of all the mammals—the nine months from mid-August to mid-May. Some of the marmots were already taking naps that lasted a day or two. Fat and drowsy, they slept longer and longer with each snooze. As they did so, their hearts beat more slowly and their bodies cooled. Eventually they would not be able to awaken until spring. Those that were still running across the rockslides whistled to one another, like children calling their dogs.

The lion tasted the wind with his tongue and nose. It tasted of another change, the change of aging and ripening. The wind bore

the scent of sweet huckleberries, ripe goose-
berries, and twinberries. This change did not
interest the mountain lion, for he was a meat
eater, or carnivore. Having looked, smelled,
and tasted, the young lion now listened. He
rotated his ears. The elk and deer had changed
their direction. They were no longer climbing
among the peaks but were moving downward.
He heard them snapping branches in the
forest below.

Since spring they had been wandering
upward toward the alpine meadows as the melting snow uncovered sweet grasses. Now the
grasses were dying, the growing season of the
high country was ending and like the birds,
the deer and elk were on migration. Their
migration, however, was not south but down
the mountain, and this concerned the lion. The
deer and elk were his staff of life. He had
moved up the mountain with them in the
spring, harvesting the weak and infirm as he

went. At about five thousand feet above sea level, where the trees stopped and the rocks, ice, and alpine prairies took over, the young lion had denned for the summer. His shelter was a twisted thicket of alpine firs, the last trees to withstand the driving wind and stunting cold at the tops of the mountains. They mark the timberline beyond which no trees grow.

Tonight the elk and deer were two thousand feet below the lion in a lower and, therefore, different kind of forest. On mountains the forests change with the altitude, the tougher trees braving the rugged heights. The lion could smell the pungent cedars the herds were trampling lower down the mountain. He must follow.

Before he entered the forest, he stopped in the last alpine meadow and tipped his ears forward. An elk had injured his foot in a crevasse several days ago and was limping through the trees, *da, thump, thump, thump.* The lion swished his tail. This animal was wounded. In the scheme of things he would falter and eventually be harvested.

Slowly the lion crossed the meadow. Beneath his feet a different sort of change was taking place. Spring was beginning. Under the leaf stems of the tiny alpine willow trees, no taller than a thumb, new buds were forming. This was happening not only on the mountain but all across the northern United States and Canada. Next year's willows, elm, maple, beech, and apple leaf buds were forming. As they emerged, the cells that brought food and water to the old leaves shut down. When these were sealed off, the leaves would lose their chlorophyll, turn yellow, red, orange, or gold and fall to the ground.

The young lion stopped at the edge of the forest and listened. He had lost sight and sound of the limping elk, so he climbed a leaning cedar to search for him. Lean and muscular, the lion was magnificently beautiful. Tawny in color, he had black smudges under his eyes and along his nose. His back was as straight as a leveling rod, his paws immense. His tail was tipped with black and almost as long as he. It touched the ground and curled up at the end. He weighed more than two hundred pounds. He was a cougar, or mountain lion, of North America. Almost as large as African lions, cougars are the second largest species of cat in the New World. Only jaguars surpass them in length and weight.

A hundred years ago mountain lions were abundant in all the mountains of the United States and Canada. Now they are rare in the United States and found only in the lonely wilderness areas of the West, Southwest, and Florida. Washington's Olympic Peninsula, a land barely touched by humans, still has its appropriate number of mountain lions. Because of their presence the elk and deer do not become so numerous that they ravage trees, bushes, grasses, and the wildlife that depend on them for shelter and food. The lions keep the herds in balance with their environment.

From the tree, the young lion could see the Hoh River Valley where he had been born and raised. Turning his head he glanced up the mountain. The snow-covered peaks of the Olympic Mountains shone like silver saw blades against the purple-black sky. In the moonlight the mountain glaciers looked like Rocky Mountain goats sleeping on the dark rocks. Some of the spots may even have been goats. The goats lived at timberline and above all year round.

The lion's sensitive ears could hear the largest glacier, Blue Glacier, moan as its tons of ice moved great boulders, slowly grinding them to dust. In the August heat, all sixty glaciers were melting. The melt spilled down the mountain, forming waterfalls, streams, and the many rivers that joined the sea.

The lion could not locate the lame elk. Silently he leaped to the ground and slipped into the forest.

Born three years ago under the August moon—lion cubs in the north arrive in spring and into the summer—the young lion had lived with his mother and two sisters in a high valley of the Hoh River. He rarely saw his father, who had remained with his mother only a short time before returning to his solitary life. He would seek out the young lion's mother again in two or three years, when the cubs were on their own. Meanwhile, like most cats, he would live alone.

After a three-month pregnancy the lioness had given birth to cubs who were about one foot long and covered with spotted fur. In ten days their eyes opened.

They were weaned in three months. By that

time the young lion had shed the spots and ringed tail of his childhood. He weighed about forty pounds and ventured out of the rock den with his mother and sisters. Together they hunted around the den, catching grouse, rabbits, and occasionally a coyote. When they were almost fully grown, they hunted farther and farther afield until they knew all about the game in their kingdom of several square miles. Eventually they were able to hunt the prey of the adult mountain lion—deer and elk. Each dawn they returned to their den.

At home they rolled and played like house cats, batting stones and flowers around, jumping on one another. Like house cats they also made many sounds, expressing different feelings.

A year ago in July the young lion had left home. He climbed out of the valley, following the deer and elk up through tall forests, over rocks, and along cliffs. After several days he came to an alpine meadow high up on Mount

Olympus where the herds grazed. No other lion ran him off the rich find, so he stayed in a twisted alpine fir forest until the moon of change drove the herds down-mountain. He went with them down almost to sea level, where the stately northern rain forests grow. Here the herds and the young lion lived all winter in a forest kept forever green by the warm rains from the sea.

One night in spring a thrilling sound brought him to his feet. A female mountain lion was calling from the other side of the Hoh River. Her scream was the high-pitched cry that the young lion recognized to be a mother cat's danger call to her cubs. He sat down and stared at the far side of the river. His whiskers stood out straight and his tail swished in anticipation.

The thin cry of a lost cub came from the riverbed. The young lion did not move. A stick snapped across the river. A lioness and two cubs slipped out from among the alder trees at the river edge and ran toward the water. The cubs were both males. The mother meowed and the lost cub ran to meet them. This one was a female—a lively cub of almost a year, who piqued the interest of the young lion. He watched her closely.

After the family was reunited, the mother led them to a log. The cubs sat down. The mother lay on her side and, reaching under the fallen tree with her strong paws, pulled out some game she had cached there. The cubs set upon it with snarls and growls. When their stomachs were round with food, the mother shoved the leftovers back under the log and, kicking leaves over it, led her tawny-colored youngsters into the eerie yellow-green forest. The young lion watched until they disappeared.

After that he was constantly on the alert for the family. Twice he heard the mother call and several times he saw the cubs. They were growing up. Their tumbles and rollicks became skilled pounces. Their thin cries developed into growls and roars. One night in June, he heard the lioness call from the northern end of her kingdom, and he saw the family no more. It was time for him to follow the elk and deer up the mountain.

Now, two months later, the moon of change was rising. The young lion was headed down-mountain again. As he went, like all cats, he climbed logs and rocks and cliffs to survey the land below. Having lost track of the limping elk, he strode to the top of a cliff to search for him. Rocks avalanched below him and once more he heard the *da, thump, thump, thump* of the limping buck. Dropping from the cliff like plunging water, he struck the earth and tracked the elk to the edge of a small lake, where he lost him. Around the lake grew blue-bells, yarrow, glacier lilies, cinquefoil, and cow parsnips. They were all blooming at once. In the lowlands some of these are spring flowers, while others are fall flowers, but in the mountains the growing season is so short that everything must bloom and go to seed between June and September. Spring's bluebells come into flower with autumn's asters.

As the lion walked around the lake, he awakened a junco who was sleeping behind a curtain of moss beneath an embankment. The bird saw the lion's shadow in the moonlight and called *tik-tik*, the danger signal of the junco. Her five youngsters, sleeping under roots and flowers nearby, awakened. They did not fly, for their mother's note warned them to tighten their feet on their perches and sit perfectly still.

The youngsters had been flying for only three days. Nevertheless, they knew where the seeds of the alpine flowers lay, and today they had learned to shell them. Tomorrow they would bathe and preen their feathers and the next day they would sun themselves, the last achievement of a baby bird before its adolescence.

Then they would start down the mountain with the elk, the deer, and the lion. They would not spend much time with them, however. When the snows came they would migrate to the lowlands of British Columbia and even as far as Mexico. Everywhere they would be known affectionately as "snowbirds," as their white tail feathers flashed over cold gray fields and under bird feeders in backyards.

The mother junco watched a starlike avalanche lily bounce above her head. When it became still, she waited and then softly called "all's well" to her family. The enemy was gone.

The young lion walked to the spillway where the lake poured over its embankment to become a stream. The stream rushed downhill forming waterfalls and pools. He listened, but the limping elk could not be heard over the sound of water. He continued down among mountain hemlocks, silver and Alaska firs, and gigantic red cedars. Pine drops and twinberries grew under these trees.

In silence the lion searched for the limping elk, who was aware of the hunter and was hiding in a dense clump of cedars not far from the lion. Sensing him, the lion climbed to a high ledge. The limping elk saw him outlined against the sky. Terrified, he dashed down-mountain to a stream at the foot of a waterfall. So soft was the floor of the forest that the lion did not hear him go.

A most remarkable bird heard the elk splash into the water. He was a dipper, or water ouzel, a small gray songbird. He peered out from behind a waterfall, where he was roosting in an air pocket, and shifted his weight from one foot to the other. He had flown there at dusk through a split in the falling water. Dippers are birds of rushing streams and falling cascades. Wild water is their home. Dry and well hidden, the wondrous bird preened his feathers until they lay so smoothly no water could seep in, then went back to sleep.

The dipper had hatched in a round nest of moss on the wall of the gorge above the cascade. He had remained there for three weeks— a long time for a songbird, which usually remains in the nest only ten to twelve days. But the longer the dipper stayed in the nest, the stronger he became. He needed to be strong because he had to fly from his nest across the raging cascade. Two weeks ago he had made the perilous flight.

Although he had landed safely and was exhausted, his parents would not let him rest. They led him right into the stream. Surprisingly, he floated on the water like a duck. His parents demonstrated how to use the swift currents to cross the raging torrent without being washed away. When he had succeeded, they led him to a quiet pool. They dove and swam underwater. The young bird hesitated, then dove. As silver bubbles passed his eyes, he instinctively pumped his wings and arrived on the bottom of the stream. There he grasped pebbles with the hooklike claws on his toes, and ran along the stream bottom. His parents gobbled the larvae of the black fly and so did the young dipper. Surfacing with them, he flew through the air and alit beside his parents on a ledge behind the cascade. There in an air pocket he rested, safe from hawk, bass, and weasel.

This night the young dipper was on his own, independent of his parents. Through the falling water he saw the young lion come to the stream. The bird was not afraid. He looked at the big cat, then stuck his beak in his feathers. Not even a mountain lion would dare to walk into the thunderous waterfall.

The lion saw the elk splash out of the stream. With a bound he followed.

Above the mountain lion, high up in the fir trees that lined the stream, slept the tiny birds of the treetops, the kinglets. They were waiting for September, when they would follow the hummingbirds south. Pine siskins, which would fly south as far as the snowbirds do, were asleep against the boles of tall trees. These small birds were of little interest to the lion. He was, however, interested in the sweet odor of the blue grouse sleeping at the edge of a cedar glen. These grouse of the Olympic Peninsula were tasty food. He crouched to catch one, but did not. The lame elk was crossing the stream again. The lion followed it downhill in deliberate pursuit.

Leaping the waterway, he ran quite a distance, then suddenly slowed down and stopped. A bull elk was pawing the ground and thrashing his huge antlers in a grassy glade. He was alone, preparing for the mating season. In September he would bugle like the monarch elk he was and call his harem to him. And he would fight all bulls who dared to come near.

The lion twisted his ears and sniffed. A large herd of elk was in a clearing above him. They were resting and browsing as they slowly worked their way down the Hoh Valley. The lion was about to stop and join their more leisurely ascent when he heard the limping elk. He was hobbling down the mountain in great fear. The lion pursued him down an elk trail and into the mysteriously beautiful northern rain forest. Here the huge Sitka spruce, western hemlock, and Douglas fir were two hundred and fifty feet tall. Their trunks were six to nine feet in diameter, and many of the trees were five hundred years old. Water-loving mosses, mushrooms, ferns, vines, and microbes grew in luxurious profusion. The lion stopped and listened. The moist vegetation hushed the forest.

He could not hear the elk. The elk was tired, and was standing only a few hundred feet away. Thirst assailed the lion, and he walked to a spring to drink. Tiny frogs, which had just emerged from their tadpole stage and come onto the land, felt his step. They leaped back into the water. Waves from their dives knocked against the lion's nose. Unwittingly a large frog hopped onto his paw, then jumped ashore. It crawled up a fern and clung there by means of the suction pads on its feet. The lion turned his head to observe it. The frog plunged back into the spring.

The lion was about to drink when he saw beside his other paw another amphibian—a northwestern hop toad. She, too, had become an adult this month. The lion lifted his paw. The toad jumped, not into the spring like the frog, but toward the woods. After spending months in the spring the toad had changed from a water-loving pollywog into a land creature. The lion reached for her playfully. The toad leaped four feet and disappeared.

Sniffing the air, the lion picked up the scent of the lame elk, now moving away. He followed him along the stream that flowed from the spring.

A great splashing in the shallows caught his attention. A large coho salmon was fighting his way, half out of water, toward a gravel bar. It was the same gravel bar where he had hatched. Now, seven years later, he was coming back to it. He had swum from the deep ocean up the Hoh River, to the feeder stream, and finally to the gravel bar where he had started his life. Here he would spawn with one of the females who were also coming home to this bar. Together the salmon would spawn and die, the last deeds of these coho salmon and millions more like them.

The lion left the salmon and followed the scent of the lame elk.

The moon was low in the western sky. Dawn would soon follow. A killdeer awoke beside the stream and flew screaming into the darkness. The lion ignored her. His hunger was beginning to gnaw at him. He wanted the elk. He climbed to the top of a bluff and saw him directly below. Crouching to pounce, he took aim.

He did not leap. Across the river something moved. Among the skyscrapers of Sitka spruce, a shadow flitted in such harmony with the forest that only the night vision of a cat could tell who walked there. A surge of warmth rushed over him. He forgot his hunger. Down the top of the cliff on the other side of the river came the child lioness and her mother. Behind them strolled one brother.

He tensed. Coming toward the family on the same trail was an enormous black bear. His head was low, his shoulder blades pumping up and down. He marched with great strength and deliberation.

Before the young lion's eyes the mother lioness and bear met. Both were surprised. Both reacted. The lioness extended her razor-sharp claws, hissed, and leaped for the bear's neck. The bear reared to his hind feet, swung his powerful front paw, and tore open the back of the lioness. He locked his teeth in her shoulder and, as he did, lost his footing on the edge of the cliff. He fell, dragging the lioness with him to the river shore forty feet below. Although they pawed at trees and branches, they could not break their plunge. They crashed to the earth. A long silence followed. Presently the bear rolled to his feet and limped away. The lioness did not get up.

With three bounds the young lion crossed the river to the lifeless cat. He caterwauled, a lonesome, bloodcurdling scream.

A leaf, as large as a dinner plate and yellow with the change of August, fell from the top of the cliff. The big maple leaf spiraled to the ground. The young lion looked up. Peering over the edge of the cliff was the child lioness. He called to her. Slowly she came down the trail on the rim of the cliff and stopped before him. He sniffed her ears and nose. They rubbed foreheads in greeting, then he led her into the rain forest.

The child lioness stayed close to the young lion's heels. Not far behind them, moving with hesitation, came the yearling brother. The young lion had a family. The orphans followed him as they had followed their mother, creating a new role for a solitary male mountain lion.

The three walked deeper into the forest. Where the trees made columned hallways, the child lioness took the lead. She led the young lion and her brother under the roots of fallen spruce, upholstered in soft club moss. She led them into a glade where lacy ferns grew everywhere—on trees, rocks, limbs, other ferns. She took them over a forest floor bright green with oxalis—a pretty wood sorrel that provides a carpet of three-leafed designs.

The child lioness led them to the foot of a moss-covered boulder. Leaping onto it, she turned and looked down at the young lion. He vaulted to her side. She crept under an enormous log covered with ferns and fragrant bedstraw. There she lay down. The brother climbed up the rock and stretched out beside her. They were home.

Lowering himself to his belly, shoulders and haunches jutting, head erect, the young lion sat sphinxlike on the rock and stared at the child lioness and her brother, not knowing quite what to do about them.

The young lion dozed in the quiet time just before dawn when the night animals are bedding down and the day animals are not yet up. He did not see the monkey flowers bob in the wind that stirs as the day breaks. He did not see the ferns absorb dew, or the wind pick up their spores and carry them away to drop and plant them. Nor did he hear the winter wren sing his morning song.

Exuberant little birds, the wrens are permanent residents of the northern rain forest. They do not migrate like the hummingbirds and swallows but stay in this environment all year. The wren sang only briefly, for it was August, and the singing and nesting seasons were over. He flew off to eat, paying no attention to the lions or the far-off drilling of a pileated woodpecker, a two-foot-high bird who was a match for the enormous trees of the rain forest.

A chickaree, a little red squirrel, scolded and announced the passing of a bobcat, a cat about a third the size of the young lion. A raven sneaked through the trees on her way to the coast to hunt mice. Then the sun came up and the lions briefly opened their eyes.

They purred to one another and went to sleep.

Dull swishing sounds in the forest marked

the homecoming of a herd of black-tailed deer. As the sun came up, they bedded down for the day. Deer feed in the predawn and at twilight. They sleep in the bright daylight and during the dark of night.

All day the lions slept, occasionally waking and purring to one another. The sun shone— a rare event in this land where ten to twelve feet of rain falls in the course of a year.

At sundown the mountain lions got to their feet. The child lioness leaped from the boulder and ran down the family trail that led to the ocean. The young lion followed. Suddenly he crouched. There was a flash of movement, and a thud. The lion had felled a deer for his family. They dined, then proceeded leisurely toward the ocean.

When the moon had waxed from a sliver to ball and waned from ball to a sliver, the three lions reached the ocean. Curious about the sea and sky, they walked the beach until the sun came up and drove them back to the shelter of the forest.

The young lion was weary of his kittens. He turned and walked away. Inland along a riverbed the first of the elk had gathered for the winter. He climbed a toppled tree six feet in diameter, waited and watched. Alone and content, he lounged in the feathery mosses and deer ferns.

The winter rainy season was upon the forest, the fog dense, and the plants dripping like chimes. He heard the child lioness call from close by. He waited. Presently she stole quietly out of the yellow-green forest and sat down on the far end of his log. He tucked his paws under his chest and stared at her. She tucked her paws under her chest and stared at him. They looked away, then back again. All night they stared and looked away.

In the darkness before dawn the lion yawned and went to hunt. The lioness arose and walked up the riverbank. Each looked back at the other. The courtship of the mountain lion had begun.

The moon of change had brought the young lion a mate.

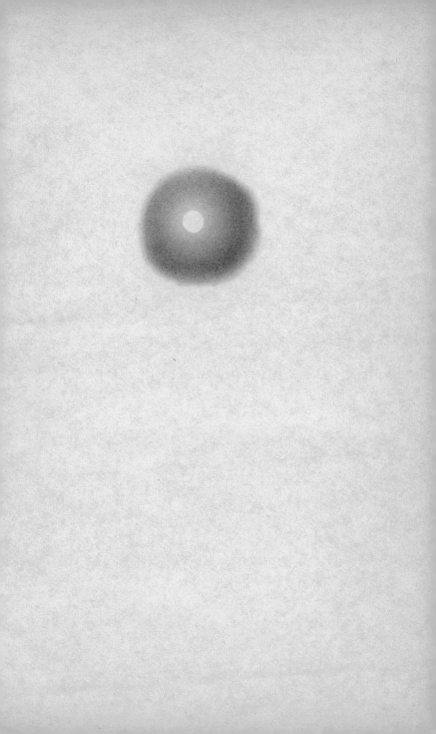

BIBLIOGRAPHY

Alcock, John. *Sonoran Desert Summer*. Tucson, Ariz.: University of Arizona Press, 1990.

Audubon, John James, and the Rev. John Bachman, D.C. *The Imperial Collection of Audubon Animals*. Maplewood, N.J.: Hammond, Inc., 1967.

Burt, Willam H., and Richard P. Grossenheider. *A Field Guide to the Mammals*. The Peterson Field Guide Series. Boston: Houghton Mifflin Company, 1976.

Carter, Anne. *Ruff Leaves Home*. New York: Crown Publishers, 1986.

Cockrum, E. Lendell. *Mammals of the Southwest*. Tucson, Ariz.: University of Arizona Press, 1982.

Gray, Robert. *Cougar, the Natural Life of a North American Mountain Lion*. New York: Grosset, 1972.

Hartley, Deborah. *Up North in Winter*. New York: E. P. Dutton, 1986.

Kjelgaard, Jim. *Haunt Fox.* New York: Holiday House, 1954.

Lavine, Sigmund A. *Wonders of Foxes.* New York: Dodd, Mead, 1986.

Leighner, Alice Mills. *Reynard.* New York: Atheneum, 1986.

Macdonald, David, ed. *The Encyclopedia of Mammals.* New York: Facts on File Inc., 1984.

MacQuitty, Miranda. *Discovering Foxes.* New York: Bookwright Press, 1988.

McDearmon, Kay. *Cougar.* New York: Dodd, Mead, 1977.

――――. *Foxes.* New York: Dodd, Mead. 1981.

Palmer, Ralph S. *The Mammal Guide.* Garden City, N.Y.: Doubleday & Company, 1954.

The Raintree Illustrated Science Encyclopedia, Vol. 13, p. 123. Milwaukee, Wis.: Raintree Publishers Ltd., 1979.

Rumsey, Marian. *Lion on the Run*. New York: Morrow, 1973.

Schneiper, Claudia. *On the Trail of the Fox*. Minneapolis, Minn.: Carolrhoda Books Inc., 1986.

Souls, Lyle K. *The Peccaries*. Tucson, Ariz.: University of Arizona Press, 1984.

Wallace, Bill. *Shadow on the Snow*. New York: Holiday House, 1985.

The World Book Encyclopedia. Vol. 7, p. 379. Chicago: World Book Inc., 1983.

The World Book Encyclopedia. Vol. 15, p. 198. Chicago: World Book Inc., 1983.

INDEX